The LAZY FRE♡CHIE

in LA

lifestyle guide for instagram lovers

Aurélie Hagen

𝕃𝕃 | LANNOO

TABLE OF CONTENTS

LIST OF PICTOGRAMS

 __ green areas - parks - squares - architecture

 __ restaurants

 __ coffee - sweets - bakeries - tea rooms

 __ ice cream

 __ bars - wine bars - cocktail bars

 __ concept stores - beauty - wellness - decoration

 __ fashion

 __ museums - bookshops

ADDRESSES

Hollywood, West Hollywood, Los Feliz, Downtown, Koreatown, Arts District, Echo Park

HOLLYWOOD

71 Griffith Observatory
2800 E Observatory Rd
@GriffithObservatory
172

59 Wanderlust
1357 N Highland Ave
@WanderlustHLWD 155

67 Friends and family
5150 Hollywood Blvd
@WeAreFriendsAndFamily
167

33 Tiago Coffee Bar + Kitchen
7080 Hollywood Blvd
@TiagoCoffee
109

58 Madison & Park Coffee
7494 Santa Monica Blvd
@MadisonAndParkCoffee 153

79 Meson Café
459 N Western Ave
@MesonCafe
193

60 Van Leeuwen Ice Cream
5915 Franklin
@VanLeeuwenIceCream
155

12 Mama Shelter
6500 Selma Ave
@MamaShelterLA
66

69 Hello Kitty Hollywood
6801 Hollywood Blvd
@HelloKittyHollywood
169

10 Urban Outfitters
1520 N Cahuenga Blvd
@UrbanOutfitters
65

82 The Daily Planet book
5931 Franklin Ave
@TheDailyPlanetBookstore
199

DOWNTOWN

46 Grand Central Market
317 S Broadway
@GrandCentralMarketLA 131

53 ROWDTLA
@RowDTLA
138 777 Alameda St Public

5

LOS FELIZ

ARTS DISTRICT

LARCHMONT VILLAGE

FAIRFAX DISTRICT

FRANKLIN VILLAGE

KOREATOWN

ECHO PARK

West Hollywood

Westwood, Brentwood, Beverly Hills, Sawtelle, West Hollywood, Century City, Venice, Santa Monica

WESTWOOD

5 Cava
1073 Broxton Ave
@ Cava
79

163
24 Native Food Café
1114 Gayley Ave
@ NativeFoodsCafe

83
6 Saffron and Rose Ice Cream
1387 Westwood Blvd
@ SaffronAndRoseIC

91
11 Paper Source
1033 Westwood Blvd
@ PaperSource

BEVERLY HILLS

1 Whole Foods
239 N Crescent Dr
@ WholeFoods
41

190
32 Beverly Hills Hotel
9641 Sunset Blvd

185
28 Soom Soom
4503, 9533 S Santa Monica Blvd
@ SoomSoomFresh

193
33 The Kind Ones
9527 S Santa Monica Blvd
@ TheKindOnes

35 Sprinkles Cupcakes
9635 S Santa Monica Blvd
@ SprinklesCupcakes
197

197
36 Joe And the Juice
9632 S Santa Monica Blvd
@ JoeAndTheJuice

75
3 Olive And June
430 N Canon Dr
@ OliveAndJune

9 Paper Source
9460 Brighton Way
@ PaperSource
89

184
29 Pottery Barn
300 N Beverly Dr
@ PotteryBarn

WEST HOLLYWOOD

CENTURY CITY

BRENTWOOD

SAWTELLE

VENICE

SANTA MONICA

Echo Park, Silver Lake

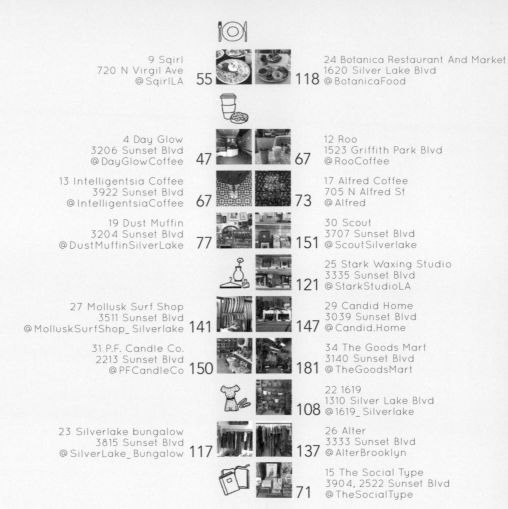

Malibu, Santa Monica, Venice, Mar Vista, Culver City

SANTA MONICA

8 Flower Child
1332 2nd St
@EatFlowerChild 45

191 48 Samosa House
2301 Main St
@SamosaHouse

149 34 Urth Caffe
2327 Main St
@UrthCaffe

199 49 Sweet Rose Creamery
826 Pico Blvd
@SweetRoseCreamery

3 Anthropologie
1402 3rd st Promenade
@Anthropologie 35

89 18 Rapha Los Angeles
1347 4th St
@Rapha

24 The Closet Trading Company
2708 Main St
@TheCloset.SantaMonica 125

191 47 Ten Women Gallery
2719 Main St
@TenWomenArtists

VENICE

181 42 Hotel Erwin
1697 Pacific Ave
@HotelErwin

32 2 The Great White
1604 Pacific Ave
@GreatWhiteVenice

12 Greenleaf
1239 Abbot Kinney Blvd
@GreenLeafChopChop 51

69 16 The Poke Shack
79 Windward Ave
@ThePokeShack

36 Gjelina
1429 Abbot Kinney Blvd
@GjelinaRestaurant 148

187 44 Zinque
600 Venice Blvd
@Zinque

45 The Butcher's Daughter
1205 Abbot Kinney Blvd
@TheButchersDaughter_Official 189

191 46 Gjusta Bakery
320 Sunset Ave
@GjustaBakery

MAR VISTA

CULVER CITY

MAPS

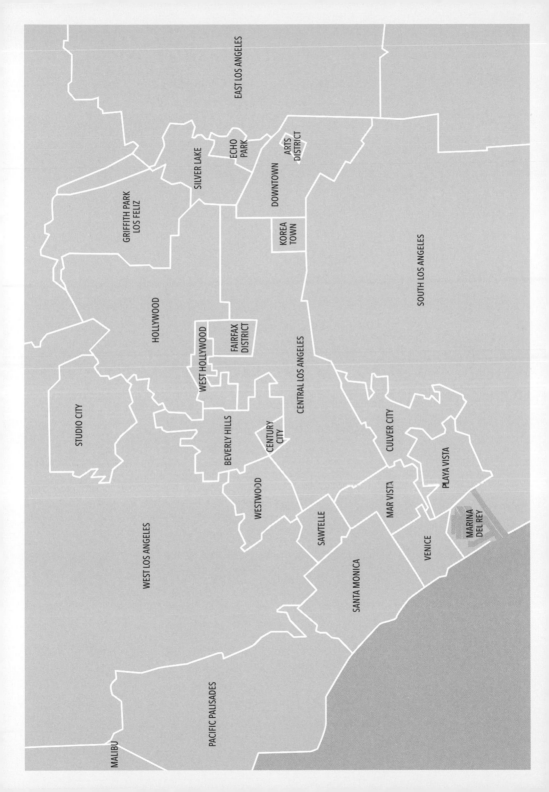

West Hollywood – Hollywood –
Los Feliz – Downtown – Koreatown –
Arts District – Echo Park

STUDIO CITY

4

60   34

82

Hollywood Blvd

33   69

76   12   10

Sunset Blvd

3   59
Fountain Avenue

38   WEST
51   25   SUNSET STRIP   HOLLYWOOD   HOLLYWOOD

NORMA TRIANGLE   58

64   Hollywood
40   Cemetery

37   79
62

41   FAIRFAX
30   45   DISTRICT   OAKWOOD
55   35   20
Beverly Blvd   48   15   31
36   32   57   56   18
Burton Way   24   27   63
BEVERLY HILLS   81   50   7   17   61

Highland Avenue

Western Avenue

26
74

23

72

47
52

Pico Blvd

Venice Blvd

Venice Blvd

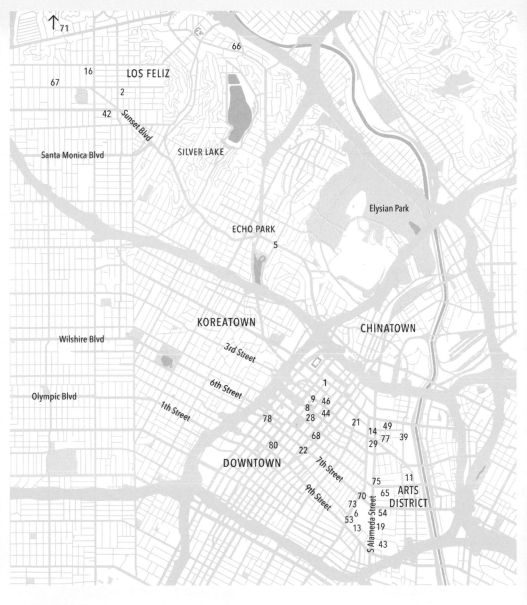

Santa Monica Blvd

LOS FELIZ

Sunset Blvd

SILVER LAKE

Elysian Park

ECHO PARK

Wilshire Blvd

KOREATOWN

CHINATOWN

3rd Street

6th Street

Olympic Blvd

1th Street

DOWNTOWN

7th Street

9th Street

ARTS DISTRICT

S Alameda Street

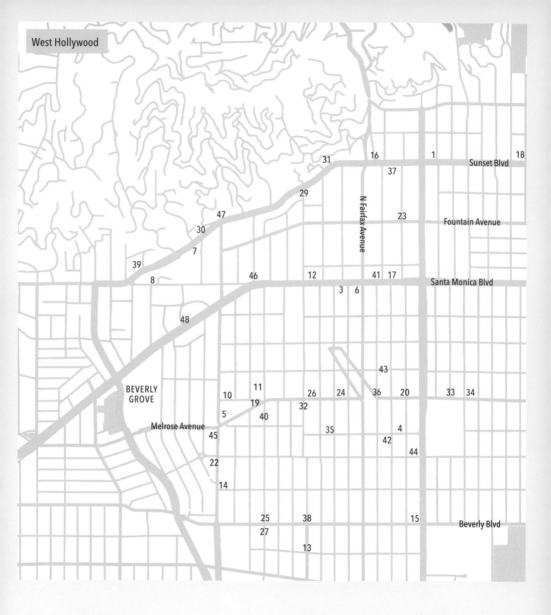

West Hollywood

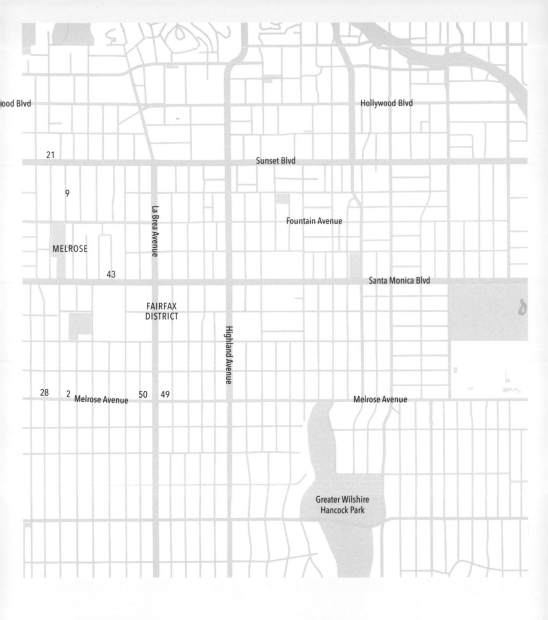

ood Blvd

Hollywood Blvd

21

Sunset Blvd

9

La Brea Avenue

Fountain Avenue

MELROSE

43

Santa Monica Blvd

FAIRFAX
DISTRICT

Highland Avenue

28 2   50 49

Melrose Avenue

Melrose Avenue

Greater Wilshire
Hancock Park

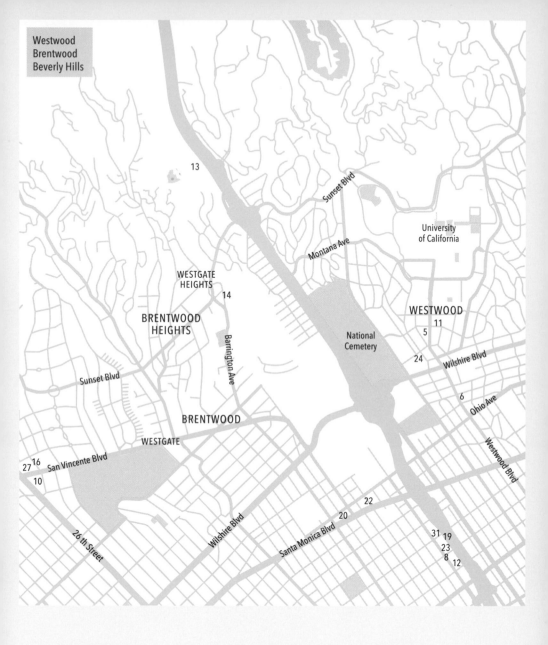

Westwood
Brentwood
Beverly Hills

University of California

WESTGATE
HEIGHTS

BRENTWOOD
HEIGHTS

National
Cemetery

WESTWOOD

Sunset Blvd

Montana Ave

Barrington Ave

Sunset Blvd

Wilshire Blvd

Ohio Ave

Westwood Blvd

BRENTWOOD

WESTGATE

San Vincente Blvd

26 th Street

Wilshire Blvd

Santa Monica Blvd

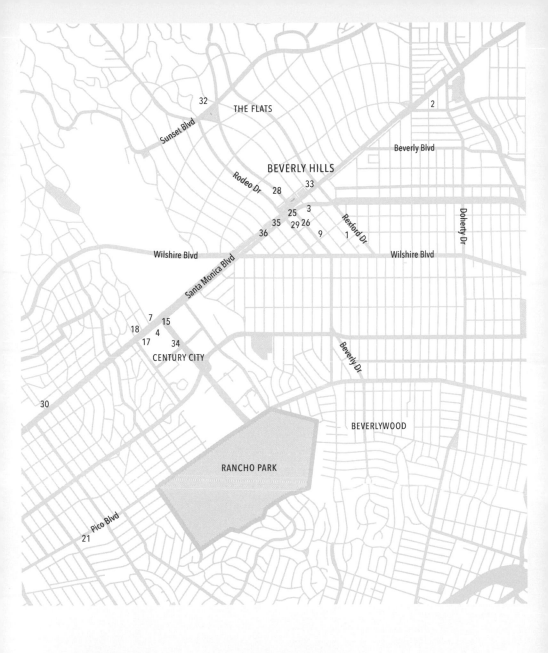

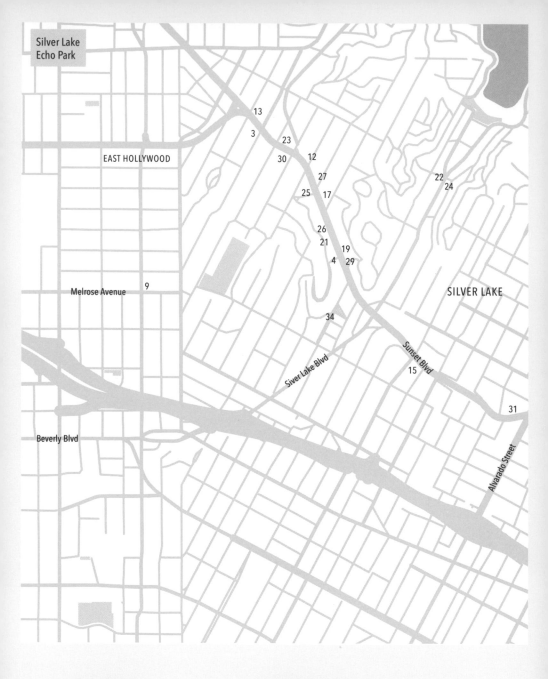

Silver Lake
Echo Park

EAST HOLLYWOOD

13
3
23
30   12
27
25   17
26
21   19
4   29
34
Melrose Avenue   9
SILVER LAKE

Siver Lake Blvd

Sunset Blvd
15
Beverly Blvd

22
24

31

Alvarado Street

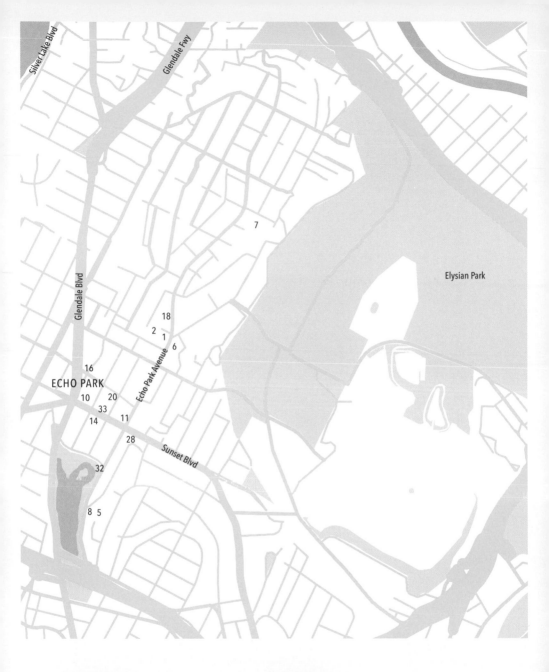

Silver Lake Blvd

Glendale Fwy

Glendale Blvd

7

Elysian Park

18

2 1

6

16

ECHO PARK

10 20

33

14 11

28

Sunset Blvd

Echo Park Avenue

32

8 5

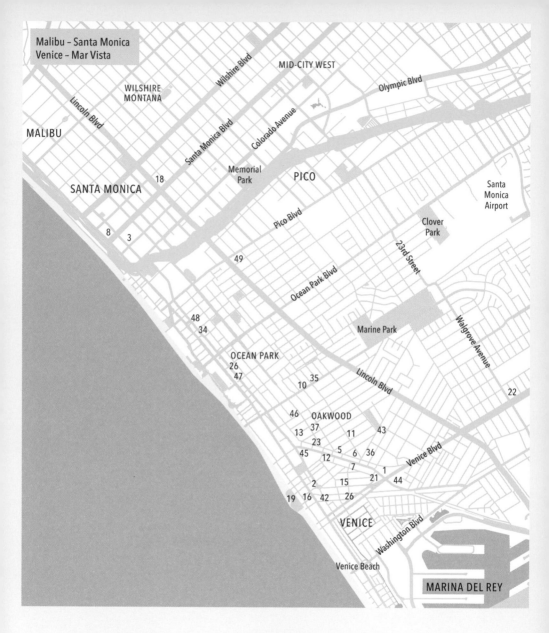

Malibu – Santa Monica
Venice – Mar Vista

MID-CITY WEST

Wilshire Blvd

Olympic Blvd

WILSHIRE
MONTANA

Lincoln Blvd

MALIBU

Santa Monica Blvd

Colorado Avenue

Memorial
Park

PICO

18

SANTA MONICA

Santa
Monica
Airport

8   3

Pico Blvd

Clover
Park

49

23rd Street

Ocean Park Blvd

Marine Park

Walgrove Avenue

48
34

OCEAN PARK
26
47

10   35

Lincoln Blvd

22

46
13   37

OAKWOOD

11   43

23

5   6   36

45   12

7

2   15   21   44

1

19   16   42   26

VENICE

Washington Blvd

Venice Beach

MARINA DEL REY

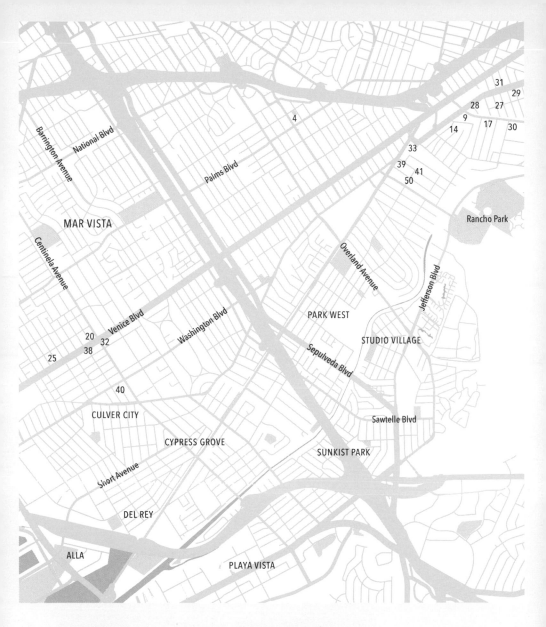

Clockwise from left:
#LifestyleBoutique at @ThePieceCollective (Venice);
#FlowerPower (Silver Lake);
#VintageBus (Hollywood);
#SpringDress (Westwood).
Opposite page:
#AcaiBowl at @GreatWhiteVenice (Venice).

Clockwise from left:
#MelroseAvenue (West Hollywood);
#IHaveThisThingWithTiles at @PaceJoint (West Hollywood);
#MugCollection at @Anthropologie (Santa Monica);
#IntoTheWild at El Matador Beach (Malibu).
Opposite Page:
#AfternoonLight (West Hollywood).

Clockwise from left:
#GiftIdeas at @Shout.And.About (Echo Park);
#WalkOfFame (Hollywood);
#FrenchPastry at @LaChouquetteOfficial (West Hollywood).
#CoffeeToGo at @CoffeeCommissary (Culver City);
Opposite Page:
#PinkDreams (Echo Park).

Clockwise from left:
#SecondHandGems at @OutOfTheCloset (West Hollywood);
#FratHouse (West Hollywood);
#FilterCoffee at @BlueBottle (Downtown);
#UrbanFashion at @Vdgn (Venice).
Opposite Page:
#VintageDenim at @Reformation (West Hollywood).

Clockwise from left:
#GrilledCheese at @HomeRestaurantLA (Los Feliz);
#MirrorMirror at @AnandaVenice (Venice);
#ISeeYou (West Hollywood);
#HalloweenSeason at @WholeFoods (Beverly Hills).
Opposite Page:
#MellowYellow (Santa Monica).

Clockwise from left:
#CeramicAndEnamelGoods at @TheGiveStore (West Hollywood);
#WelcomeHome (West Hollywood);
#EatWell at @CookBookMarket (Echo Park);
#CoffeeBreak at @Toms (Venice).
Opposite Page:
#UrbanOasis at #Echo Park Lake (Echo Park).

Clockwise from left:
#CaliforniaBreakfast at the @CroftAlley (West Hollywood);
#FlowersEverywhere (Echo Park);
#CeramicTiles (West Hollywood);
#MotherEarthBowl at @EatFlowerChild (Santa Monica).
Opposite Page:
#SeasonalFood at @HaydenWineBar (Culver City).

LAUREL HARDWARE

$15
Frosé
château la coste 'bellugue' rosé, ketel one botanicals & pamplemousse

$16
Gangster
tito cucumber vodka, fresh juiced watermelon & lime

LAUREL HARDWARE

SUNDAY – FRIDAY
4PM to 7PM DRINKS
4PM to 7PM FOOD

SATURDAY

BITES	5	• MARINATED OLIVES ROSEMARY BREADSTICKS
		• HAND CUT FRIES SMOKED PEPPER AIOLI
		• WILD ARUGULA SALAD BALSAMIC, PARMESAN
	10	• LOLLIPOP SPROUTS PARMESAN, RANCH
		• HEIRLOOM TOMATO BURRATA, FOCACCIA
		• GLAZED PORK RIBS GOCHUJANG, CILANTRO
		• MARGHERITA PIZZA BASIL, TOMATO
		• CLASSIC PIZZA PEPPERONI, JALAPEÑO
BEVERAGES	**DRAFT BEER** 5	• ALLAGASH WHITE
		• HOUSE BEER
		• LOST COAST TANGERINE
		• BOOMTOWN BREWERY LIMELIGHT IPA
		• MODELO ESPECIAL MEXICAN LAGER
		• GUINNESS DRAUGHT
		• REKORDERLIG SWEDISH HARD CIDER
	COCKTAILS 10	• LH MARGARITA
		• GANGSTER
		• LH MOMOTARO
	WINE BY THE GLASS 10	CHÂTEAU LA COSTE
		• RED – GRENACHE BLEND
		'LES PENTES ROUGE'
		• WHITE – VERMENTINO, SAUVIGNON BLANC
		'LES PENTES DOUCES'
		• ROSÉ – GRENACHE, SYRAH, CINSAULT
		'BELLUGUE'
		SPARKLING ROSÉ – COL DE SOLIE

Clockwise from left:
#TheUsualSunset (West Hollywood);
#TrashyLA (West Hollywood);
#CaffeineAddiction at @LaColombeCoffee (Silver Lake);
#AllYouNeedIsPink and #Coffee at @DayGlowCoffee (Silver Lake).
Opposite Page:
#AfterworkDrinks at @Laurel_Harware (West Hollywood).

Clockwise from left:
#VeganDelight at @CafeGratitude (Venice);
#DontCross (Venice);
#WhiteHouse (West Hollywood);
#MassageDay at @Equinox (West Hollywood).
Opposite Page:
#SwanLake at @WheelFunRentalsOfficial (Echo Park).

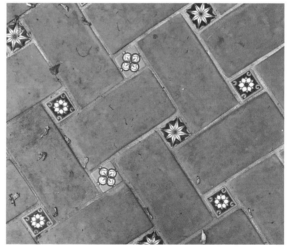

Clockwise from left:
#MorningFuel at @IntelligentsiaCoffee (Venice);
#SaladBowl at @GreenLeafChopChop (Venice);
#SpanishTiles (West Hollywood);
#SummerEssentials at @TavinBoutique (Echo Park).
Opposite Page:
#CactusParadise at @HotCactus_LA (Echo Park).

Clockwise from left:
#SummerInTheCity (Echo Park);
#FlowerVan by @TheUnlikelyFlorist (Venice);
#CaliforniaGarden (Santa Monica);
#LunchByTheLake at @BeaconEchoPark (Echo Park).
Opposite Page:
#IHaveThisThingWithTiles at @TocayaOrganica (West Hollywood).

Clockwise from left:
#CrispyRice at @SqirlLA (Silver Lake);
#DonutTime (West Hollywood);
#BrazilianBracelets (Santa Monica);
#BikingByTheBeach (Venice).
Opposite Page:
#LaVieEnRose (Echo Park).

Clockwise from left:
#LifestyleBooksAndDecor at @Poketo (Culver City);
#RamenDinner at @UrbanRamenLA (West Hollywood);
#SanctuaryAtSoledad at @TheGroveLA (West Hollywood);
#SecretStairs at #Melrose Place (West Hollywood).
Opposite Page:
#VintageRollerSkates at @SundaysBestThrift (Echo Park).

Clockwise from left:
#Palmtrees (Mar Vista);
#CherryBlossom (Los Feliz);
#ColorfulClothing at @BigBudPress (Echo Park);
#RollsRoyce on #Sunset Plaza (West Hollywood).
Opposite Page:
#VeniceCanals (Venice).

Clockwise from left:
#AmericanMailbox (West Hollywood);
#CoffeeRoastedInSantaCruz at @VerveCoffee (West Hollywood);
#JapanesePaperGoods at @HighTideStore_DTLA (Downtown);
#ClockTower (West Hollywood).
Opposite Page:
#BaywatchStyle (Santa Monica).

Clockwise from left:
#OutisdeLunch at @Dinette.LA (Echo Park);
#FashionFavorites at @Madewell (West Hollywood);
#ParkingView (Santa Monica);
#CharmingBookstore at @TheLastBookstoreLA (Downtown).
Opposite Page:
#GiftShop at @FoldDTLA (Downtown).

Clockwise from left:
#CaliHouse (Beverly Hills);
#OrangeSunset (West Hollywood);
#NeonLights at @UrbanOutfitters (Hollywood);
#CutestBoutique @BurroGoods (Venice).
Opposite Page:
#SundayBrunch at @ZincCafeAndMarket (Arts District).

Clockwise from left:
#ForTheLoveOfTiles at @IntelligentsiaCoffee (Silver Lake);
#YellowHouse (Venice);
#ColorfulHomeDecor at @ShopYolk (Downtown);
#AustralianVibe at @RooCoffee (Silver Lake).
Opposite Page:
#SunsetDrinks at @MamaShelterLA (Hollywood).

Clockwise from left:
#CuteFashion and #CuteDog at @GingerlyWitty (Echo Park);
#HawaiianFood at @ThePokeShack (Venice);
#RainbowJuices at @MoonJuice (West Hollywood);
#IHaveThisThingWithDoors (Venice).
Opposite Page:
#JustSmile by @JimmyPaintz (West Hollywood).

Clockwise from left:
#PaperGoods at @TheSocialType (Silver Lake);
#ColdBrew at @VanillaBlackLA (Echo Park);
#DreamyColors (Venice);
#ChillingInTheSun (Venice).
Opposite Page:
#VictorianHouse on #CarrollAvenue (Echo Park).

Clockwise from left:
#ButFirstCoffee at @Alfred (Silver Lake);
#VintageCar (West Hollywood);
#NewYorkStylePizza at @RobertasPizza (Culver City);
#EatHealthy at @GlowingJuices (Echo Park).
Opposite Page:
#VintageNeonSign (Silver Lake).

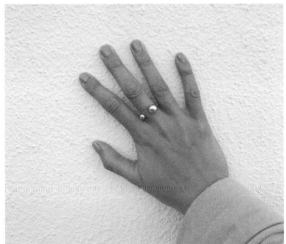

Clockwise from left:
#NeighborhoodStroll (West Hollywood);
#BubbleTea at @AlfredTea (West Hollywood);
#ManiTime at @OliveAndJune (Beverly Hills);
#LAGarden (West Hollywood).
Opposite Page:
#OceanView (Santa Monica).

Clockwise from left:
#ApparelAndDecor at @The.House.Of.Woo (Arts District);
#EnchantingGifts at @DustMuffinSilverLake (Silver Lake);
#ThaiFusion at @BangingBasil (West Hollywood);
#DelicateScents at @FreshBeauty (Century City).
Opposite Page:
#MintTea at @GGETLA (Larchmont Village).

Clockwise from left:
#MediterraneanBowl at @Cava (Westwood);
#ArtBooks at @SkylightBooks (Los Feliz);
#SpanishColonialRevival House (West Hollywood);
#AcaiBowl at @BackyardBowls (West Hollywood).
Opposite Page:
#CaliArchi (Silver Lake).

Clockwise from left:
#YellowHouse (Silver Lake);
#SucculentsLove at @TheGroveLa (West Hollywood);
#CaliforniaBowl at @RealFoodDaily (West Hollywood);
#ThisIsHalloween (Silver Lake).
Opposite Page:
#VeganThaiFood at @ArayasPlace (West Hollywood).

Clockwise from left:
#VegetarianBurger at @VeggieGrill (West Hollywood);
#AfternoonLight (West Hollywood);
#CasualStyles at @MovintNYC (Larchmont Village);
#RoseIceCream at @SaffronAndRoseIC (Westwood).
Opposite Page:
#SchoolBus (Brentwood).

Clockwise from left:
#GardeningParadise at @ShopTerrain (Century City);
#GreenOnGreen (West Hollywood);
#BeachfrontLiving (Santa Monica),
#FavoriteRamen at @TatsuRamen (Sawtelle).
Opposite Page:
#CeramicArt (West Hollywood).

Clockwise from left:

#ComfortBreakfast at @Scrumptious_Cafe_And_Bakery
(West Hollywood);

#ChillingOnTheStreet (West Hollywood);

#LatteTime at @CafeDulceLA (Downtown);

#AdventureCar (Silver Lake).

Opposite Page:

#PeaceHeaven at @ElderberriesCafe (West Hollywood).

Clockwise from left:
#GiftWrapping at @PaperSource (Beverly Hills);
#EspressoBarInACyclingStore at @Rapha (Santa Monica);
#TheGreenDoor (Beverly Hills);
#CandiesAndChocolate at @EdelweissChocolates (Brentwood).
Opposite Page:
#HoneyLavenderIceCream at @SaltAndStraw (Larchmont Village).

Clockwise from left:
#MakeUpEssentials at @Glossier (West Hollywood);
#KawaiiLove at @JapanLALittleTokyo (Downtown);
#CuteGifts at @PaperSource (Westwood);
#Latte at @Menottis (Venice).
Opposite Page:
#PinkLight (West Hollywood).

Clockwise from left:

#CactusGarden (Hollywood);

#Espresso at @PointFive_ (West Hollywood);

#FlowerPower at @WildLivingFoods (Downtown);

#Selfeet at @RepubliqueLA (Fairfax District).

Opposite Page:

#CoffeeCup at @BlueStoneLane (West Hollywood).

Clockwise from left:
#HealthyBreakfast at @BlackWoodCoffeeBar (West Hollywood);
#CreamPuffs at @BeardPapas (Sawtelle);
#BeyondTheFence (Hollywood);
#MagazineStand at @BookSoup (West Hollywood).
Opposite Page:
#CityView at @GettyMuseum (Brentwood).

Clockwise from left:
#GrilledCheese at @MonsieurMarcelFM (West Hollywood);
#SunsetLight (West Hollywood);
#WomenClothing at @ShopMarketLA (Brentwood);
#IslandBeauty (Echo Park).
Opposite Page:
#ChocolateIceCream at @JenisIceCreams (Larchmont Village).

Clockwise from left:
#NeighborhoodBookShop at @StoriesBooksAndCafe (Echo Park);
#RooftopDrinks at @PerchLosAngeles (Downtown);
#TrafficJam (Silver Lake);
#UrbanJungle (Hollywood).
Opposite Page:
#ThaiFood at @NTmrkt (Silver Lake).

Clockwise from left:
#DesignerFashion at @OpeningCeremony (West Hollywood);
#LatteArt at @CarreraCafe (West Hollywood).
#LocalBeers at @ArtsDistrictBrewing (Arts District);
#CoffeeBreak at @Cafelf.Co (West Hollywood);
Opposite Page:
#SportsWear at @RipNDip (Fairfax District).

Clockwise from left:
#PinkFlowers (Echo Park);
#KidsParadise by @BestGiftStoreEver (West Hollywood);
#CuteFacade (West Hollywood);
#SkinCareSince1851 at @Kiehls (Century City).
Opposite Page:
#ComeInRightMeow at @PaulSmith (West Hollywood).

Clockwise from left:
#Vintage2CV (West Hollywood);
#Cookbooks at @PickettFences (Larchmont Village);
#ReadLocal at @DieselBookstore (Brentwood);
#NaturalBeautyProducts at @TheDetoxMarket (West Hollywood).
Opposite Page:
#HomeDecorAndJewelry at @OkTheStore (West Hollywood).

Clockwise from left:
#FromHomeWithLove (West Hollywood);
#PinkAndShiny at @SpitFireGirlRocks (West Hollywood);
#Fountain (Hollywood);
#LifeInTurquoise (West Hollywood).
Opposite Page:
#DrinksByThePool at @TheStandard (West Hollywood).

Clockwise from left:
#Westfalia (Hollywood);
#FilterCoffee at @TiagoCoffee (Hollywood);
#CactusEverywhere (West Hollywood);
#BooksAndRecords at @CounterpointRecordsAndBooks (Franklin Village).
Opposite Page:
#VintageAndPlants at @1619_Silverlake (Silver Lake).

Clockwise from left:
#MansionLife (West Hollywood);
#MeetMeInTheHills (West Hollywood);
#CuteFashion at @Aritzia (Century City);
#AglioEOlioPasta at @JonAndVinnyDelivery (Fairfax District).
Opposite Page:
#ChocolateAndCaramelPie at @WinstonPies (West Hollywood).

Clockwise from left:
#GrilledCheeseForLife at @MelsDriveIn (West Hollywood);
#StreetArt (Beverly Hills);
#EndOfTheAfternoon (Culver City);
#ItalianFood at @EatalyLA (Century City).
Opposite Page:
#BreakfastDelight at @HedleysRestaurant (West Hollywood).

Clockwise from left:
#MexicanFood at @PinkTaco (West Hollywood);
#BeTheStar (Hollywood);
#CoffeeInTheBackyard at @AlanasCoffee (Mar Vista);
#Cactus(Culver City).
Opposite Page:
#TheUsualSunset (Venice).

Clockwise from left:
#FunkyFashion at @VivienneWestwood (West Hollywood);
#PinkHouse (Silver Lake);
#SummerDresses at @SilverLake_Bungalow (Silver Lake);
#CaliPalmtrees (Hollywood).
Opposite Page:
#BasketBallCourt (Fairfax District).

Clockwise from left:
#BehindThoseDoors (West Hollywood);
#NYCStyleArchi (Hollywood);
#AvoToast at @DialogCafe (West Hollywood);
#CastleLife (Fairfax District).
Opposite Page:
#HealthyLiving at @BotanicaFood (Silver Lake).

Clockwise from left:
#LifeInColors at @GrowVenice (Venice);
#PurpleLove (Silver Lake);
#FunGifts at @StarkStudioLA (Silver Lake);
#InTheBushes (Silver Lake).
Opposite Page:
#MelroseAvenueStyle at @ThePopUpShopLA (West Hollywood).

TARO

HONEYDEW

SESAME

PISTACHIO

MATCHA

NO MILK

HOUSE MILK

$0.50

HEMP MILK

SOY MILK

$0.50

HONEY BOBA   LYCHEE JELLY

                GRASS JELLY

ALOE   EGG PUDDING

CHIA SEEDS   SEA SALT CREAM

Clockwise from left:
#ToteBags and #Menswear at @CommonGallery (Arts District);
#Candles and #HomeDecor at @WhimsyAndRow (Culver City);
#LeatherGoods at @Cuyana (Venice);
#MinimalistLatte at @TheAssemblyCafe (West Hollywood).
Opposite Page:
#BobaTea at @PearlsFinestTeas (Fairfax District).

Clockwise from left:
#ThriftShopping at @TheCloset.SantaMonica (Santa Monica);
#LittleMouse at @TortoiseGeneralStore (Culver City);
#LunchTime at @KismetLosAngeles (Los Feliz);
#CoffeeInStyle at @MyBSweet (Sawtelle).
Opposite Page:
#PotteryClasses at @Still_Life_Ceramics (Downtown).

Clockwise from left:
#CreepyOrNotCreepy at @MelroseTradingPost (West Hollywood);
#FreshJuice at @PressBrothers (Downtown);
#SunsetTime (West Hollywood);
#HandmadeHomeGoods at @TumbleweedAndDandelion (Venice).
Opposite Page:
#VeganBrunch at @CrossroadsKitchen (West Hollywood).

Clockwise from left:

#LoveIsEverywhere (Echo Park);

#VintagePickUp (Silver Lake);

#FashionAndHomeGoods at @Midland_Shop (Culver City);

#KidsAccessories at @BurroGoods (Venice).

Opposite page:

#AuthenticDeliFood at @Canters_Deli (Fairfax District).

Clockwise from left:
#FoodMarket at @GrandCentralMarketLA (Downtown);
#LoveKey (Arts District);
#Sunset and #JunkFood (West Hollywood);
#JasmineMilkTea at @Percolate_Tea (West Hollywood).
Opposite Page:
#FiftiesDiner at @Cafe50WestLA (Sawtelle).

Clockwise from left:
#PershingSquare (Downtown);
#CutestSoySauce at @Koreatown_Plaza (Koreatown);
#WineShopAndClasses at @HelensWines (Fairfax District);
#ColorfulMakeUp at @SmashBoxCosmetics (Venice).
Opposite Page:
#MexicanFood at @Pinches_Tacos (Culver City).

Clockwise from left:

#DoubleDoor (West Hollywood);

#AmeliePoulain (West Hollywood);

#CactusForLife (Hollywood);

#VeganCheese made by a French Guy at @Vromages
(West Hollywood).

Opposite Page:

#SeasonalCuisine at @ManuelaDTLA (Downtown).

Clockwise from left:
#HistoricBrentwoodVillageTower (Brentwood);
#FrenchFood at @LittleNextDoor (West Hollywood);
#NYCFashion at @AlterBrooklyn (Silver Lake);
#DishesAndHomeDecor at @WestElm (West Hollywood).
Opposite Page:
#90210 (Beverly Hills).

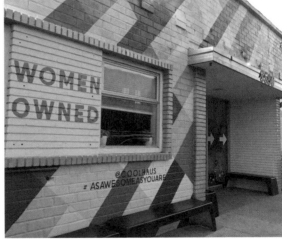

Clockwise from left:
#GroceryStore (Koreatown);
#LegendaryVenue at @TheRoxy (West Hollywood);
#CaliforniaIceCream at @Coolhaus (Culver City);
#PlantBasedBurger at @MontysGoodBurger (Koreatown).
Opposite Page:
#StreetArt at @RowDTLA (Downtown).

Clockwise from left:
#SurfInUSA at @MolluskSurfShop_Silverlake (Silver Lake);
#ArtBooks at @ArcanaBooks (Culver City);
#VintageNeonSign at @HelmsBakeryDistrict (Culver City);
#BreakfastAllDay at @CroftAlley in @TheStandard (West Hollywood).
Opposite Page:
#AlleyOfPalmTrees (Beverly Hills).

Clockwise from left:
#EthicalFashion at @GalerieLA (Downtown);
#ArtSupplies at @BlickArtMaterials (Sawtelle);
#ButternutSoup at @BBCMCafe (West Hollywood);
#LimitedEditionFashion at @SupremeNewYork (Fairfax District).
Opposite Page:
#KittyChewingGum at @Mitsuwa_MarketPlace (Mar Vista).

Clockwise from left:

#MorningFuel at @WoodCatCoffee (Echo Park);

#FlowerPower (Santa Monica);

#RainbowFacade (West Hollywood);

#SunsetOnTheSunsetStrip (Hollywood).

Opposite Page:

#TruffleBurger at @UmamiBurger (West Hollywood).

Clockwise from left:
#HollywoodSign (Hollywood);
#WindyWeather (Echo Park);
#HomeGoods at @Candid.Home (Silver Lake);
#MosaicArt (Silver Lake).
Opposite Page:
#FlatironInLA at the @Culver_Hotel (Culver City).

Clockwise from left:
#ComePickMeUp (Hollywood);
#OrganicCoffee at @UrthCaffe (Santa Monica);
#CoolestVintage at @SundaysBestThrift (Echo Park);
#YummyIceCream at @JenisIceCreams (Venice).
Opposite Page:
#PizzaLunchBreak at @GjelinaRestaurant (Venice).

Clockwise from left:
#UrbanJungle (Hollywood);
#GrilledCheeseOnBrioche at @SweetLadyJaneBakeryCafe
(West Hollywood);
#Cute2CV (West Hollywood);
#CoffeeAndGoodies at @ScoutSilverlake (Silver Lake).
Opposite Page:
#LAMadeCandles at @PFCandleCo (Echo Park).

Clockwise from left:
#GiftIdeas at @BlackMarket_LA (Sawtelle);
#IndianFood at @BadmaashLA (Fairfax District);
#CozyCoffeeBreak at @MadisonAndParkCoffee (Hollywood);
#LoveAdvice by @ProtectYoHeart (West Hollywood).
Opposite Page:
#LAVibe (Koreatown).

Clockwise from left:
#Shakshuka at @WanderlustHLWD (Hollywood);
#PinkSunset (West Hollywood);
#BoySmellsCandles at @CandleDelirium (West Hollywood);
#Coffee and #IceCream at @VanLeeuwenIceCream (Hollywood).
Opposite Page:
#Cronut at @189ByDominiqueAnsel (West Hollywood).

Clockwise from left:
#BlackBeanBurger at @GMWeHo (West Hollywood);
#TropicalFlowers (West Hollywood);
#SeventiesInspiredClothing at @AviatorNation (Venice);
#EnjoyingTheSun (West Hollywood).
Opposite Page:
#BreakfastTaco at @TacosTuMadre (Larchmont Village).

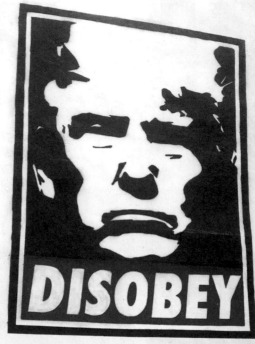

DISOBEY

@PLASTICJESUS

Plastic Jesus.

Clockwise from left:
#BlueHouse on #BlueSky (Echo Park);
#PlantsAndFashion at @ScoutLA (West Hollywood);
#RodeoDrive (Beverly Hills);
#SaladTrio at @FoodLabLA (West Hollywood).
Opposite Page:
#Disobey by @PlasticJesus (Los Feliz).

Clockwise from left:
#HealthyFreeze at @PressedJuicery (West Hollywood);
#HistoricNeighborhood (Downtown);
#CountrysideVibe (Hollywood);
#SneakersParadise at @FlightClub (Fairfax District).
Opposite Page:
#UsedAndNewBooks at @TheLastBookstoreLA (Downtown).

Clockwise from left:
#BBQSalad at @NativeFoodsCafe (Westwood);
#CaliStreetStyle (Fairfax District);
#StoreExclusives at @NikeLosAngeles (West Hollywood);
#BreakfastInAJar at @EggSlut (Venice).
Opposite Page:
#GoodMorningCalifornia (Silver Lake).

Clockwise from left:
#CandlesAndFragrances at @LuckyScent (Dowtown);
#NeighborhoodView (Silver Lake);
#BuildYourOwnBreakfast at @HugosRestaurants (West Hollywood);
#LateAfternoonLight (Culver City).
Opposite Page:
#TofuScramble and #VeganSliders at @LittlePineRestaurant
(Los Feliz).

Clockwise from left:

#TastyBreakfast at @WeAreFriendsAndFamily (Hollywood);

#CubanCoffee at @DFCasaCubana (Downtown);

#HillyStreets (Echo Park);

#CuteFashion at @ClubMonaco (Beverly Hills).

Opposite Page:

#WildWildPalmtrees (West Hollywood).

Clockwise from left:
#SanrioGems at @HelloKittyHollywood (Hollywood);
#SeeYouLater (West Hollywood);
#ColorfulClothingandDecor at @Myrtle (Downtown);
#LAHighSchool (Hollywood).
Opposite Page:
#OldSchoolBarberShop (Echo Park).

Clockwise from left:
#FunnyGiftIdeas at @826LA (Mar Vista);
#MovieTheater at @ArcLightCinemas (Culver City);
#ViewOnTheHills (Hoolywood);
#WelcomeHome (West Hollywood).
Opposite Page:
#MassamanRedCurry at @HoneyHi (Echo Park).

Clockwise from left:
#SunsetAtTheBeach (Venice);
#VintageVan (Echo Park);
#VeganTunaMelt at @TheKindSage (Echo Park);
#WildStreets (West Hollywood).
Opposite Page:
#CityView from @GriffithObservatory (Hollywood).

Clockwise from left:
#GorgeouslyGorgeous (Mar Vista);
#FlatWhite at @HaveSomeCoffeeLA (Koreatown);
#IceCreamAndPops at @GingersDivine (Culver City);
#CactusBouquet (West Hollywood).
Opposite Page:
#AvocadoToastAndSmoothie at @MakeOutEveryDay (Culver City).

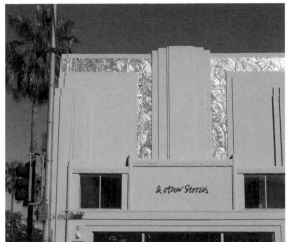

Clockwise from left:
#GoldenFacade at @AndOtherStories (Beverly Hills);
#TileArt (Mar Vista);
#PalaceLife (Downtown);
#ShadesOfBlue (Hollywood).
Opposite Page:
#BlueOnBlue (Koreatown).

Clockwise from left:
#VintageChevrolet (West Hollwyood);
#SkateParkByTheBeach (Venice);
#DesignHomeDecor at @HawkinsNewYork (Downtown);
#FireEscape (Arts District).
Opposite Page:
#RosemaryCarrotTartine at @YarrowCafe (Fairfax District).

Clockwise from left:
#EverythingForYourCocktails at @FlaskAndField (Downtown);
#QuickSnack at @TheGoodsMart (Silver Lake);
#DrinksWithAView at @HotelErwin (Venice);
#AvocadoWaffleSandwich at @MetHerAtTheBar (Fairfax District).
Opposite Page:
#SilverLakeReservoir (Silver Lake).

Clockwise from left:

#GourmetFood at @FarmShopCA (Santa Monica);

#PinkLove (West Hollywood);

#EssentialOils at @SajeWelness (Venice);

#ArmyOfTrees (West Hollywood).

Opposite Page:

#CherryBlossom (Downtown).

Clockwise from left:
#CharmedHouse (Echo Park);
#DenimHeadToToe (Downtown);
#FalafelPlate at @SoomSoomFresh (Beverly Hills);
#DreamFlowers (Echo Park).
Opposite Page:
#ChrismasDonutOrnament at @PotteryBarn (Beverly Hills).

Clockwise from left:
#AvocadoTartine at @Zinque (Venice);
#LifeByTheCanals (Venice);
#FrenchFood at @CafeChezMarie (Century City);
#StraightToTheSky (Hollywood).
Opposite Page:
#HotelRosslyn (Downtown).

Clockwise from left:
#SweetAndSavoryPies at @ThePieHoleLA (Arts District);
#JuicePassion at @TheButchersDaughter_Official (Venice);
#SneakersAndStreetWear at @Kith (West Hollywood);
#CosyCocktailLounge at @LibraryBarLA (Downtown).
Opposite Page:
#CoffeeAndTreats at @ChitChatLA (Sawtelle).

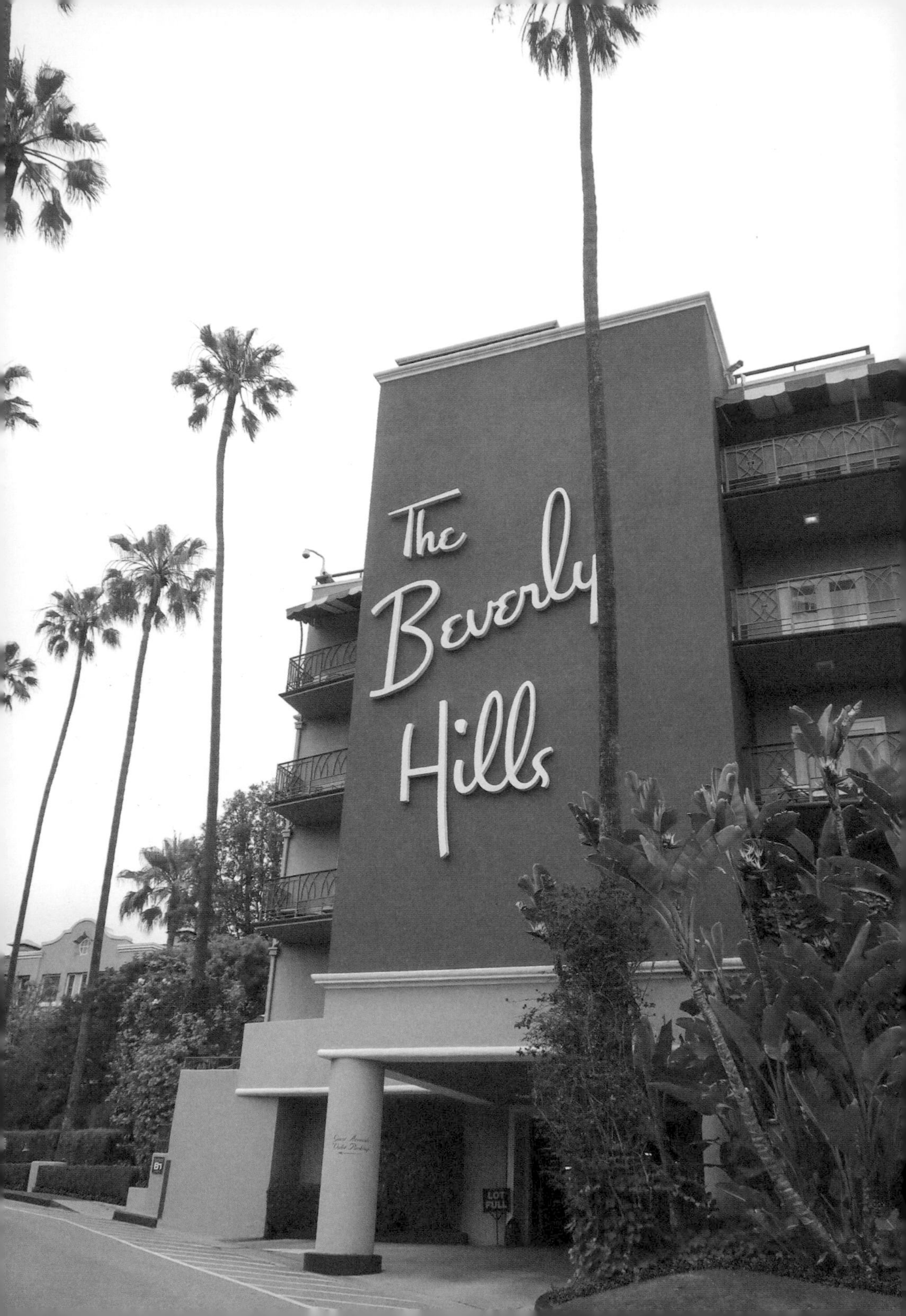
The Beverly Hills
LOT FULL

Clockwise from left:
#EarthyBowl at @GjustaBakery (Venice),
#LocalArtbyWomen at @TenWomenArtists (Santa Monica);
#AcaiBowls at @RawberriOfficial (West Hollywood);
#VegetarianIndianFood at @SamosaHouse (Santa Monica).
Opposite Page:
#FancyAfternoon at the #BeverlyHillsHotel (Beverly Hills).

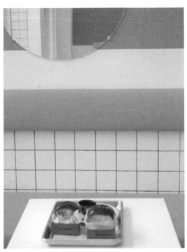

Clockwise from left:
#LatteAllDay at @Coffee.ForSasquatch (West Hollywood);
#HalloumiSandwich at @TheKindOnes (Beverly Hills);
#PanPacificPark (West Hollywood);
#BuddhaBowl at @MesonCafe (Hollywood).
Opposite Page:
#BeachView at #PalisadesPark (Santa Monica).

Clockwise from left:
#BetterHaveMyMoney (Hollywood);
#CutestLibrary (Santa Monica);
#ChocolateDelish at @BacoMercat (Downtown);
#ParadiseBirds (Hollywood).
Opposite Page:
#AlwaysProud (West Hollywood).

Clockwise from left:
#CupcakeATM by @SprinklesCupcakes (Beverly Hills);
#FavoriteDumplings at @DinTaiFungUSA (Century City);
#UrbanOasis at #SantaMonicaCommunityGarden (Santa Monica),
#AvocadoShake at @JoeAndTheJuice (Beverly Hills).
Opposite Page:
#CerealIceCream at @MilkBarStore (West Hollywood).

Clockwise from left:
#HomemadeIceCream at @SweetRoseCreamery (Santa Monica);
#EggplantSandwich at @Jaffa.LA (West Hollywood);
#ColorfulHouses (Santa Monica);
#BooksAndGifts at @TheDailyPlanetBookstore (Hollywood).
Opposite Page:
#WallpaperFacade at @PaliSociety (Culver City).

Acknowledgements

Zack, thank you for eating all these delicious meals with me and going on endless walks under the Californian sun.

Mom, even if you still hate travelling, thank you for your unconditional support in all my crazy adventures.

Thank you to Michelle for your trust since day one. Thank you to Gunther, Anne, Véronique, Alexandra, Lorrie, Lina and everybody at Racine.

Vali, thank you for being there in all the good moments but also in the most doubtful ones.

Thank you to Elise (@LosAngelesOffRoad) for taking this colorful picture of me (page 98).

Much love to the following: Vanessa, Geoffrey, Lou, Margot, Léon, Laet, Carole, Pam, Audrey, Flo, Véro, all my dear friends from Brussels, Rachel, Stefanie, Cindy, Talie, Anne, Marine, Marion, Julie, Kim, Enora, Benjamin, Gaëlle, Alix, AM, Tiffany, Granny, the Bird, GJ, Philippe, la Team Paillettes, la Team SIBP, la Team Club Med and everybody else I love very much.

All photographies: © Aurélie Hagen
Layout: Aurélie Hagen, Alexandra Jean, Véronique Lux
Cartes : Véronique Lux
Logo *The Lazy Frenchie*: Alexia Roux

This book is published by Éditions Racine.
Éditions Racine is part of the Lannoo Publishing Group.

If you have any questions or comments about the material in this book, please do not hesitate to contact our editorial team: michelle.poskin@racine.be

The publisher and the author has made every effort to trace the proprietors of the copyright of the images printed herein in accordance with the law. The publisher welcomes any correspondence from copyright holders they were unable to contact.

Instagram is a trademark of Instagram LLC, which does not sponsor, authorize, or endorse this book.

© Éditions Racine, 2019
Tour et Taxis, Entrepôt royal
86C, Avenue du Port, BP 104A · B - 1000 Brussels

www.racine.be
Register for our newsletter to receive information regularly on our publications and activities.

D/2019/6852/15
Legal deposit: August 2019
ISBN 978-2-39025-099-9
Printed in Serbia